posh®
Coloring
BOOK
SOOTHING DESIGNS
FOR FUN & RELAXATION
Andrews McMeel Publishing®
a division of Andrews McMeel Universal

W9-AAC-483

POSH® COLORING BOOK
SOOTHING DESIGNS FOR FUN & RELAXATION

copyright © 2015 by Michael O'Mara Books Limited. All rights reserved. Printed in the United States of America. No part of this book may be used or reproduced in any manner whatsoever without written permission except in the case of reprints in the context of reviews.

Andrews McMeel Publishing
a division of Andrews McMeel Universal
1130 Walnut Street, Kansas City, Missouri 64106

www.andrewsmcmeel.com

16 17 18 19 20 MLY 15 14 13 12 11 10 9

ISBN: 978-1-4494-7200-9

Illustrations by Angela Porter, Angelea Van Dam, Cathy Chhetri, Claire Cater, Hannah Davies, Rosalind Monks, Sally Moret, and Textile Candy.

ATTENTION: SCHOOLS AND BUSINESSES
Andrews McMeel books are available at quantity discounts with bulk purchase for educational, business, or sales promotional use. For information, please e-mail the Andrews McMeel Publishing Special Sales Department: specialsales@amuniversal.com.

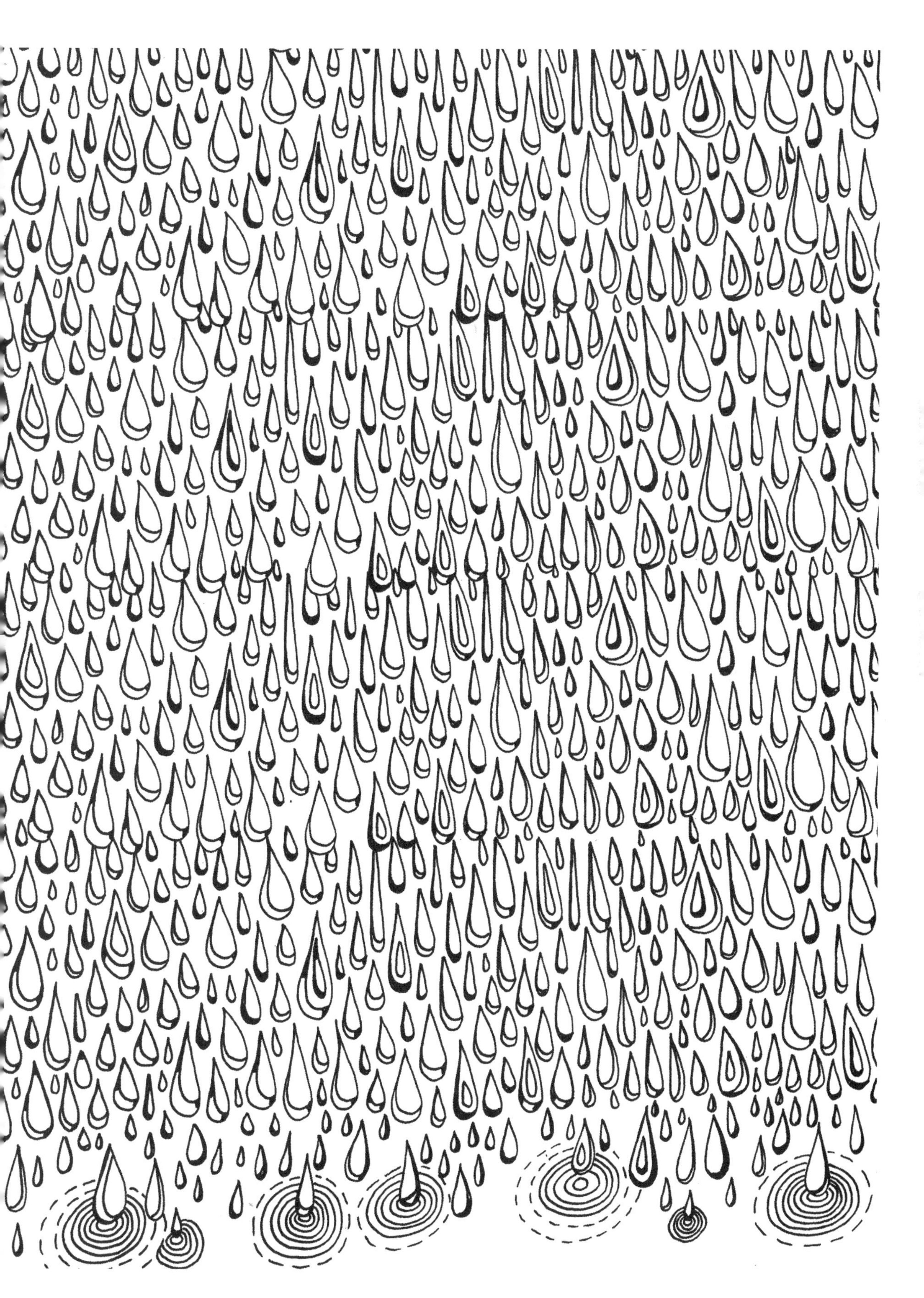

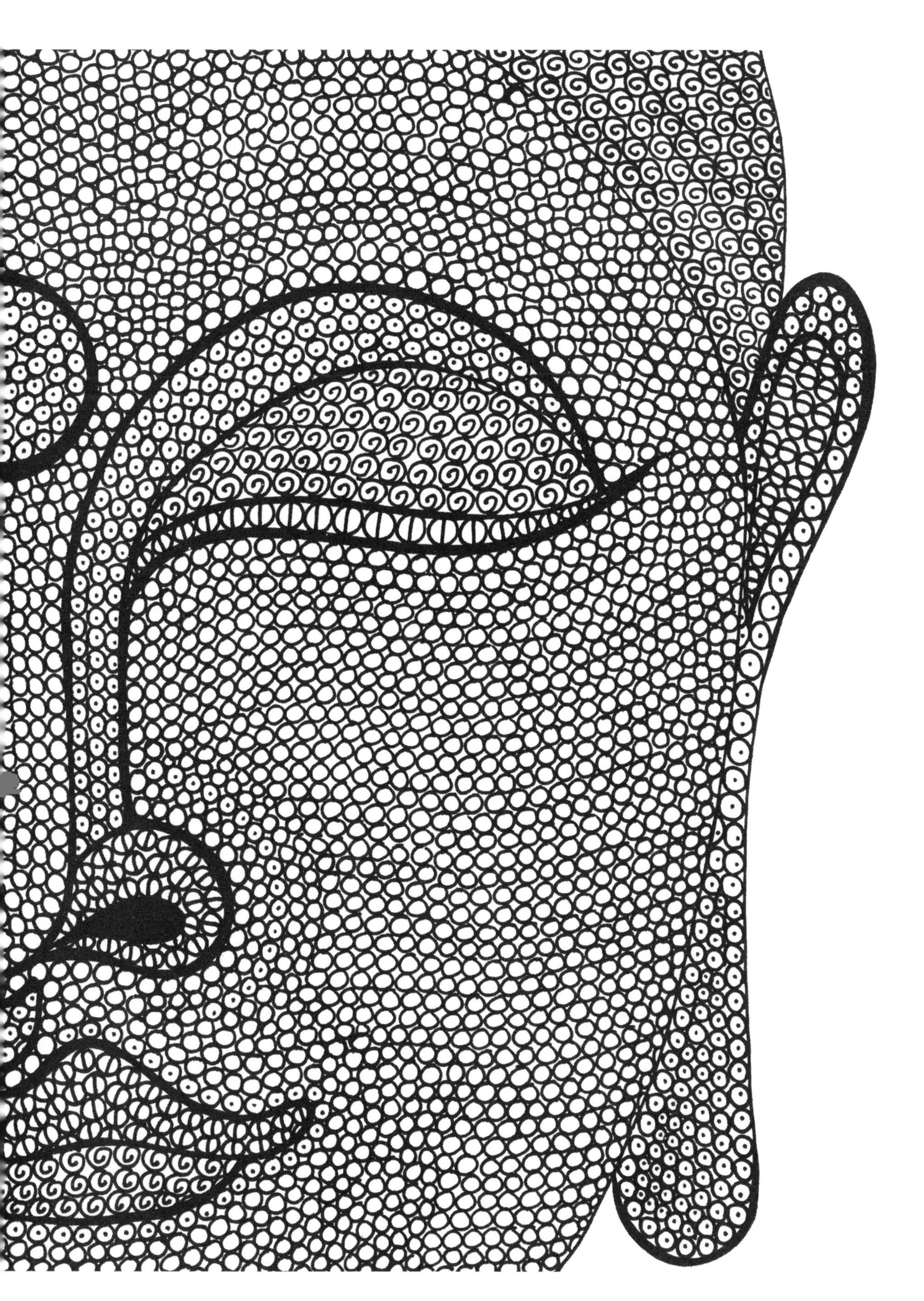

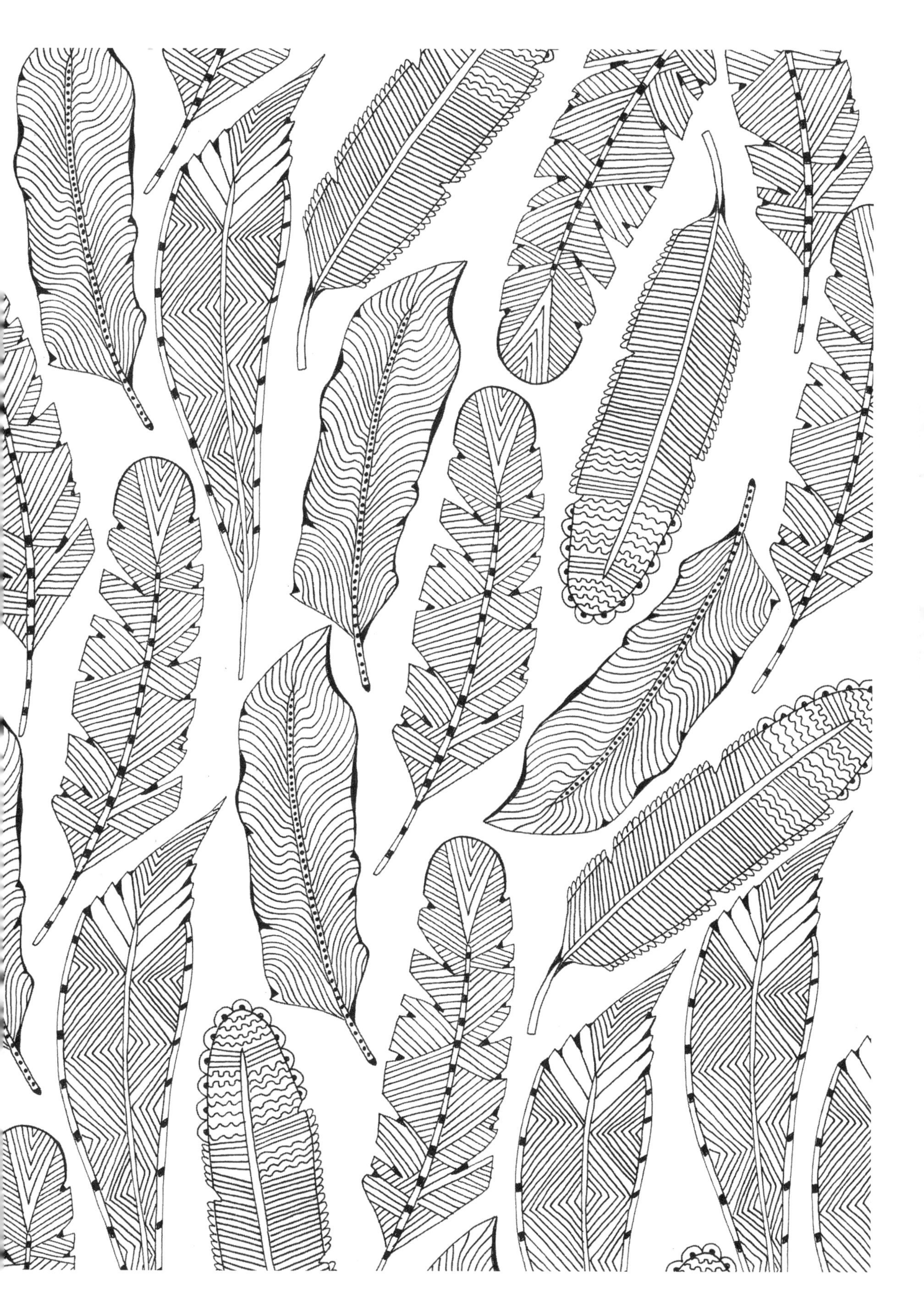

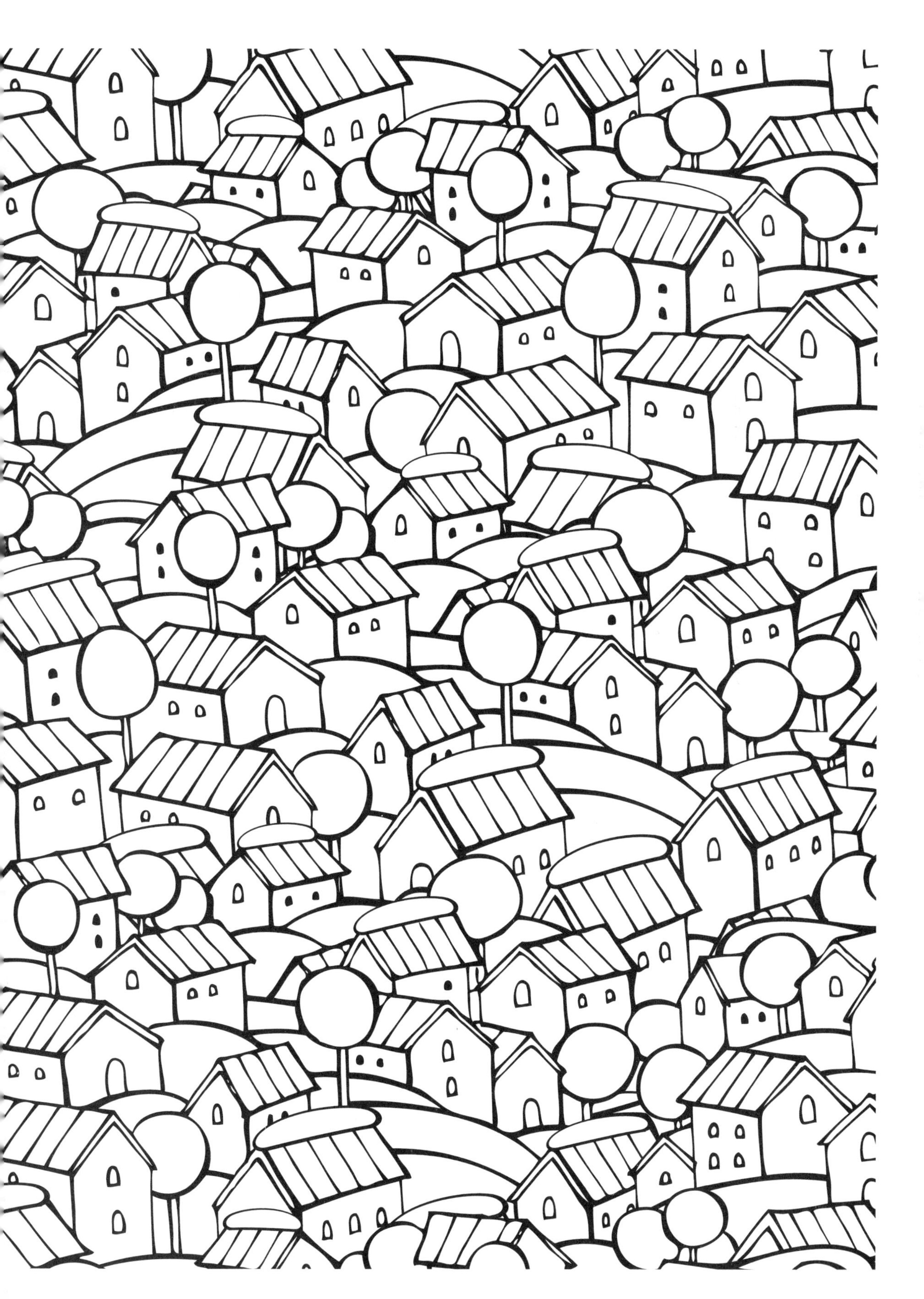

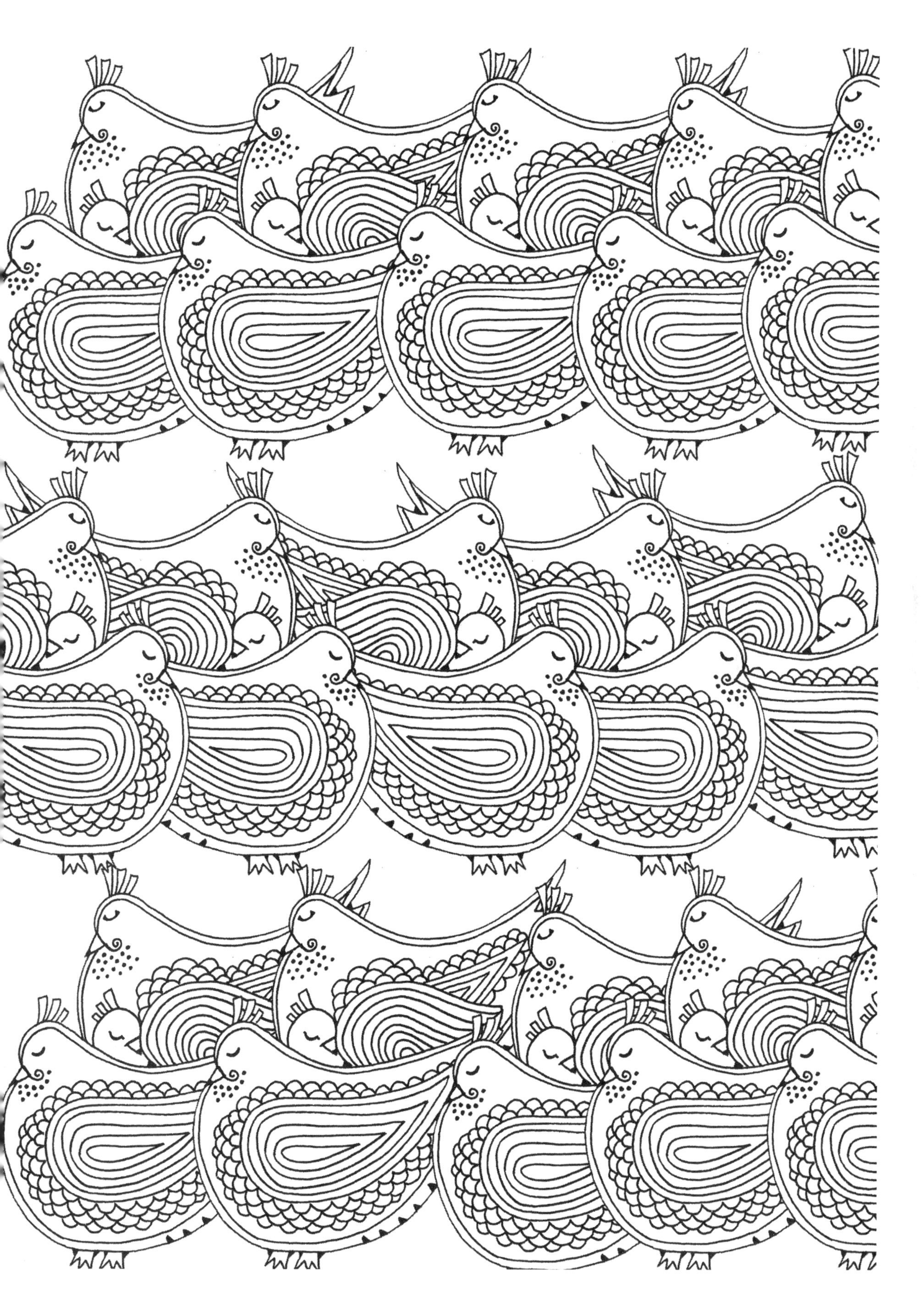

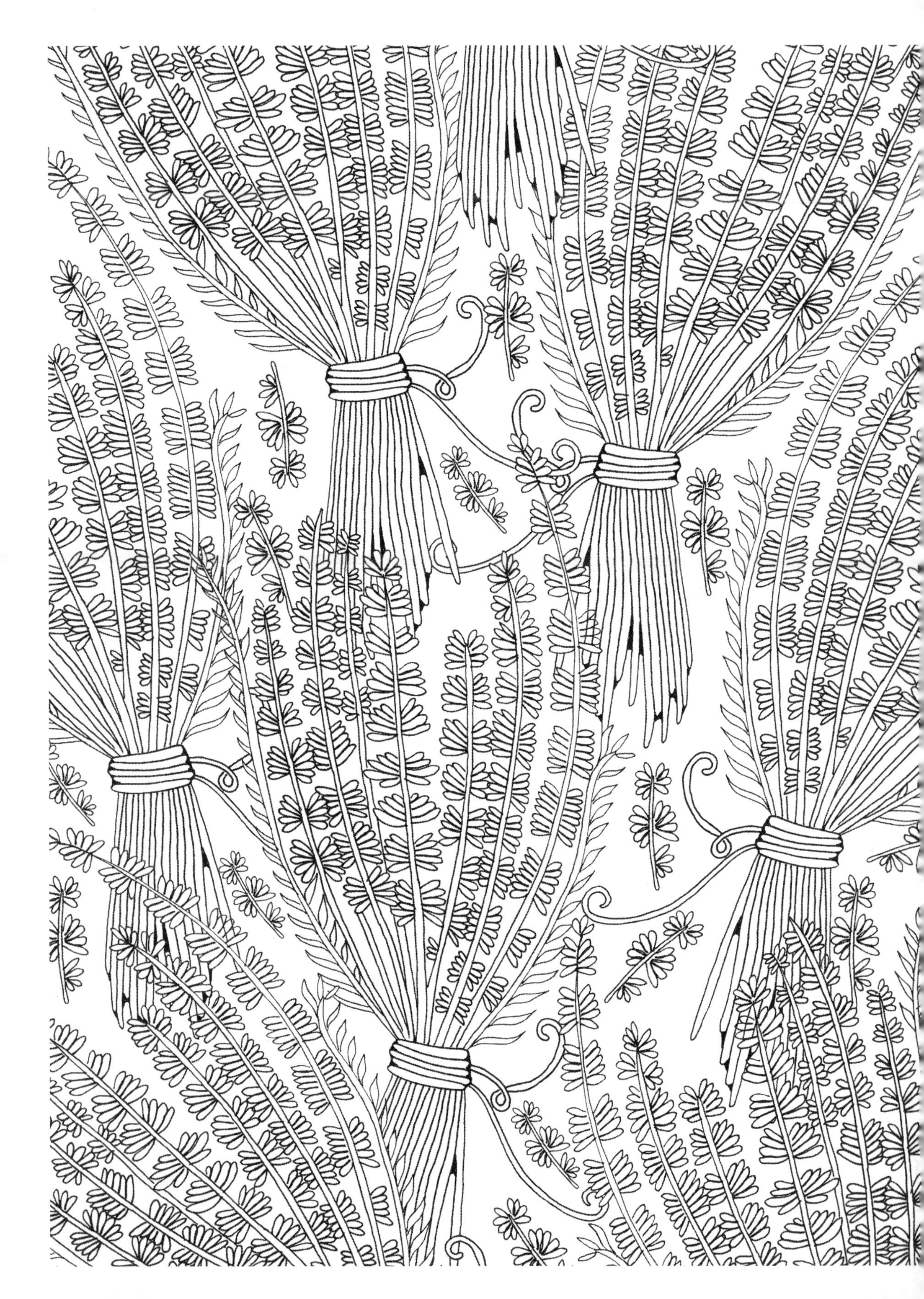

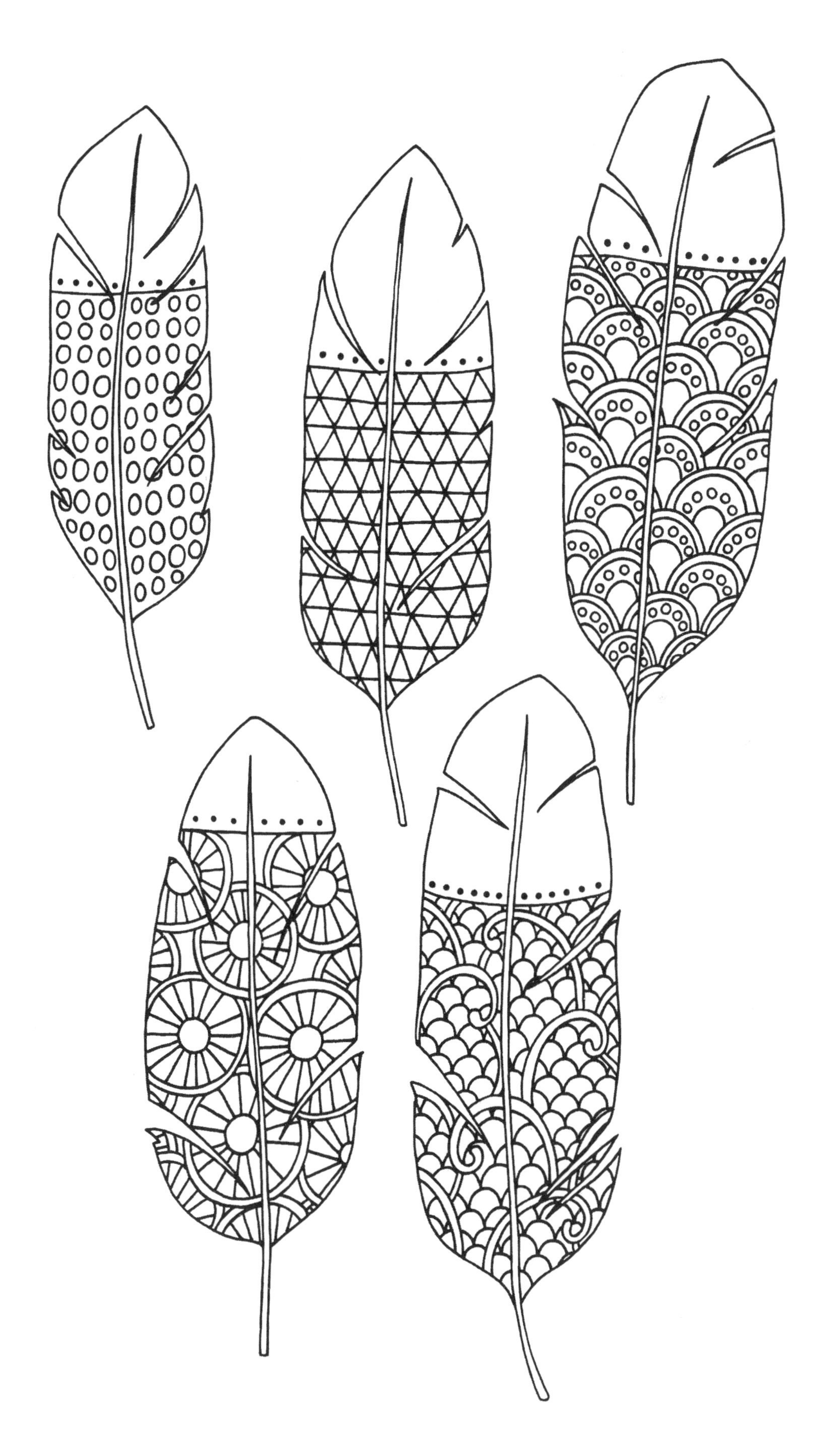